汉语桥-中学生夏令营
Chinese Bridge Summer Camp for Foreign Students

中国欢迎你 Welcome to China 短期汉语系列教材

国家汉办/孔子学院总部
Hanban / Confucius Institute Headquarters

Xue Taoyi
学陶艺
Ceramics

才艺类

高等教育出版社·北京
HIGHER EDUCATION PRESS BEIJING

“中国欢迎你”短期汉语系列教材

总策划　许　琳

总监制　王永利

策　划　陈　默　　邵亦鹏

监　制　薛　佼

编委会成员（按姓名音序排列）

常　春	迟兰英	代凝慧	丁　磊	丁　颖	董　赟
范祖奎	冯丽君	郝永宁	贺红梅	侯晓彬	纪仁盛
贾静芳	贾腾飞	姜志琪	金飞飞	鞠　慧	孔庆国
孔雪晴	李红艳	李　娜	梁小岸	梁　云	刘芳珍
刘玉波	卢小燕	罗来莉	罗兴平	孟宪滨	秦晓燕
屠晓蓓	汪正才	王　岱	王文龙	王　艳	王　瑜
王玉静	温　培	吴玉为	席忠祥	许　娟	杨　硕
杨晓霞	袁　勇	张　蕾	张　丽	张全生	张新江
张　勇	章新拓	赵江民	郑　颖	周　芳	周　荧
朱　璇	朱　芸				

前言

随着中国与世界各国距离的拉近，越来越多的人渴望了解中国、体验中国。为了帮助“汉语桥”夏令营中小学生以及所有对中国感兴趣的外国朋友在较短时间内了解中国的语言和文化、历史与风俗，中国国家汉办/孔子学院总部组织研发了“中国欢迎你”短期汉语系列教材。

◎ 适用对象

本系列教材主要适用于来华参加夏令营的海外中小学生，也可用于海外孔子学院和孔子课堂作为汉语教学辅助资源。

◎ 教材构成

本系列教材分为三大类：语言类、才艺类和地域类。

《学陶艺》是才艺类教材中的一册，主要内容包括陶艺基本知识、陶瓷作品欣赏、陶艺基本技法、陶艺制作等。本书将文化与才艺学习有机地结合起来，同时配以丰富的练习和活动，目的在于帮助学习者在较短时间内了解中国陶瓷的基本知识，掌握手工陶艺的基本制作技能。本书的参考教学时间为6～8学时。

◎ 编写特色

1. 全新的编写理念：本系列教材借鉴了全新的外语教学理念和最先进的外语教学法成果，真正做到以学习者为中心，满足学习者的个性化需求。

2. 全新的编写风格：本系列教材话题实用，内容简单，形式丰富，图文并茂，寓教于乐，注重实效，目的在于使汉语变得“易懂、易学、易用”。

3. 全新的教学设计：本系列教材以任务和活动为主线，便于教师进行教学设计，充分调动学习者的兴趣，实现轻松有效的课堂教学。

让我们翻开书，一起去感知充满魅力的汉语和中国文化！

编委会

2011年5月

Ceramics
陶艺

Contents 目录

Introduction to Ceramics
陶艺介绍

The term "ceramics" includes both pottery and porcelain. Pottery figures of Han Dynasty and Tri-color glazed pottery are the representative works of Chinese ceramics.

The invention of porcelain is based on the constant development and improvement of pottery-making technology. Porcelain originated in China and so far, porcelain has a history of over 3 000 years. In English, the word "China" stands for the "country" and "china" means "porcelain." Exquisite ancient Chinese porcelain not only has superb craftsmanship and unique beauty, but it also contains the essence of ancient Chinese painting, calligraphy, sculpture, and other art forms. Porcelain has become a favorite item for the world's major museums and art collectors.

陶瓷包括陶器和瓷器。汉代的陶俑、唐代的唐三彩等都是中国陶器的代表作。

瓷器的发明是在陶器技术不断发展和提高的基础上产生的。众所周知，瓷器的故乡在中国，迄今已有三千多年的历史。英文China大写表示“中国”，小写则表示“瓷器”。精美的中国古代瓷器不仅包含高超的制作技艺和独特的美感，而且包含中国古代绘画、书法、雕刻等艺术的精髓，现已成为世界各大博物馆和艺术收藏家们竞相收藏的珍品。

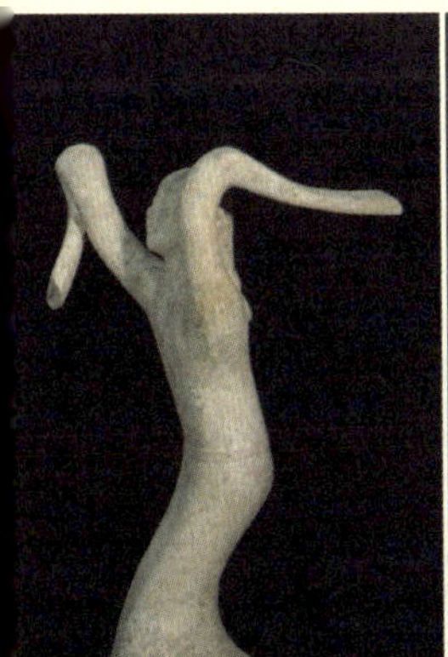

代陶俑
ttery figures of Han
nasty

唐三彩
Tri-color glazed pottery

秦始皇陵兵马俑
The Terracotta Warriors

True or False? 判断正误

1. China was the first country in which porcelain was invented. ( )
中国是最先发明瓷器的国家。
2. Tri-color glazed pottery of the Han Dynasty is representative of Chinese ceramics. ( )
汉代的唐三彩是中国陶器的代表作。
3. The invention of porcelain and pottery was at almost the same time. ( )
瓷器和陶器是同时发明的。

Knowledge Links 知识链接

Tri-colored glazed pottery is a kind of pottery popular in the Tang Dynasty, with yellow, white and green as the basic colors.

唐三彩：是一种盛行于唐代的陶器，以黄、白、绿为基本色。

Blue-and-white porcelain, also called "blue and white porcelain with the white background" or simply "blue flower," is one of the major categories of porcelain in ancient China.

青花瓷：又称"白地青花瓷"，简称"青花"，是中国古代瓷器的主流品种之一。

Jingdezhen is located in northeast of Jiangxi Province and is renowned as China's "capital of porcelain."

景德镇：位于江西东北部，被称为中国的"瓷都"。

The Beauty of Ceramics
陶瓷作品欣赏

There is a wide variety of ceramics which are diverse in style and fully embody people's imagination and creativity.

陶瓷种类繁多，风格多样，充分展现了古人的想象力和创造力。

人面鱼纹彩陶盆
距今大约5000～7000年

Painted pottery basin with a human face and fish pattern, about 5000-7000 years old.

宋代绿定熏香
公元10～12世纪

Perfume pot of the Song Dynasty, 10th-12th century.

秦始皇兵马俑一号坑
公元前3世纪

First Dig of the terracotta warriors in Mausoleum of First Emperor of the Qin Dynasty, 3rd century BC.

唐三彩腾空马俑
公元7～10世纪

Tri-color glazed pottery of the galloping horse, 7th-10th century.

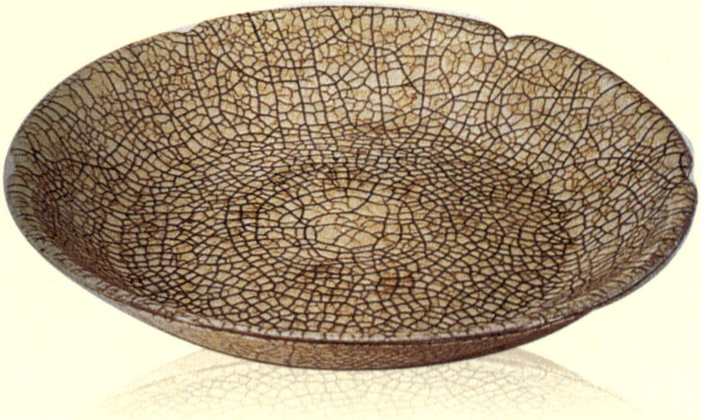

南宋哥窑米黄釉葵瓣口盘
公元12～13世纪
Porcelain plate of the Southern Song Dynasty, 12th–13th century.

清代粉彩八宝纹盘
公元19世纪
Porcelain plate of the Qing Dynasty, 19th century.

明代五彩鱼藻文罐
公元16世纪
Fish-pattern porcelain jar of the Ming Dynasty, 16th century.

黑陶蛋壳杯
距今大约3950～4350年
Egg-shaped black pottery cup, about 3950–4350 years old.

明代青花执壶
公元15世纪
Blue-and-white porcelain pot of the Ming Dynasty, 15th century.

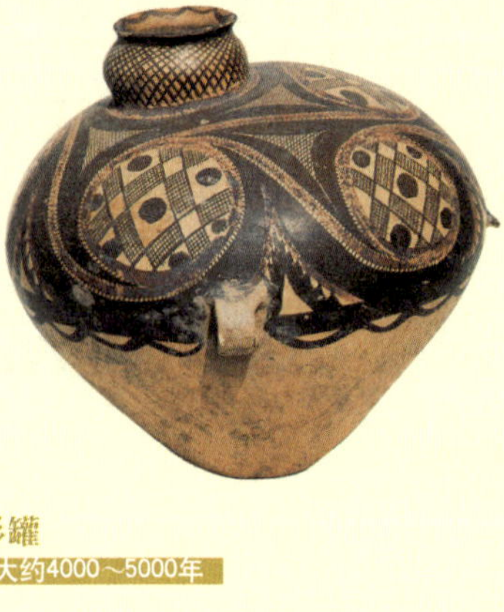

鸟形罐
距今大约4000～5000年
Bird-shape pottery jar, about 4000–5000 years old.

Ceramic Making 制陶方法

1. Making the mould: form the raw material into the desired shape.
   制坯：将原料制成一定的形状。

   Made by hand
   手工制作

   Made by machine
   机器拉坯

2. Drying: dry the item.
   风干：晾干坯体。

3. Repairing: repair the item to make it smooth, uniformly thick, and decorate it with designs.
   修坯：修整坯体使它表面光滑、厚薄均匀，并加以绘画装饰。

4. Glazing: paint glaze onto the surface of the item.
   上釉：在坯体表面涂上釉浆。

5. Firing: control the baking temperature.
   烧制：控温烧制。

Let's Think 想一想

Guess which of the following characteristics belong to pottery and which belong to porcelain. Learn to differentiate pottery and porcelain.

猜一猜，下面哪些特点是陶器的，哪些是瓷器的。在老师的指导下，学着辨认一下陶器和瓷器。

以瓷土为原料（　） uses porcelain clay as raw material	烧制温度较高（　） high firing temperature	敲击声音发闷（　） low-pitched sound if tapped	不透明（　） opaque
以陶土为原料（　） uses pottery clay as raw material	烧制温度较低（　） low firing temperature	敲击声音清脆（　） clear, crisp sound when tapped	半透明（　） translucent

Making Ceramics
陶艺制作

手工陶艺的基本技法 Basic Techniques of Ceramic Art

1 捏 niē pinch	2 揉 róu knead
3 贴 tiē stick	4 刻划 kēhuā carve
5 镂空 lòukōng hollow	6 压 yā press
7 搓 cuō twine	8 盘筑 pánzhù roll

Try It Yourself 试一试

1. Can you tell what techniques were used in the work on the right?
   你能看出右图中的作品使用了以上哪些技法吗？
2. Carve your Chinese name onto a piece of clay board.
   试着在泥板上刻出自己的中文名字。
3. Choose any three of the above techniques and create your own work using your imagination. See whose work is the most distinctive.
   任意选择三种技法，发挥想象，完成一件作品。比一比谁的作品最有特点。
4. Form groups. Each group make 10 pottery bowls of the same size. See which group does the best job.
   几人一组，每组做十个大小相等的陶碗。看看哪组做得又快又好。

Make a Pottery Fish
制作陶鱼

玉鱼
Jade fish

剪纸
Paper-cut

年画
Spring Festival picture

鱼盘
Fish plate

鱼灯
Fish lantern

瓦当
Eaves-tile

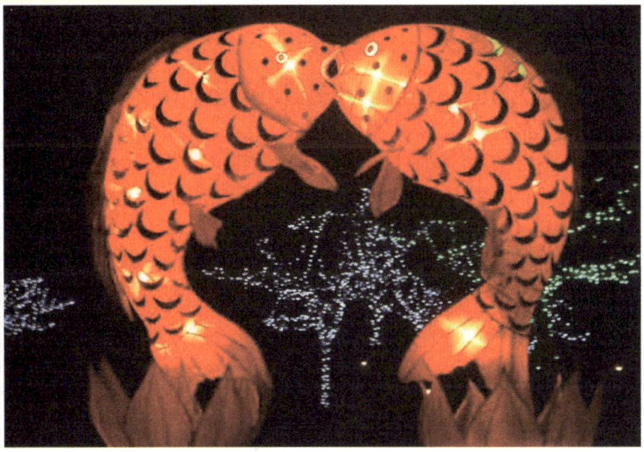

Chinese people think that the fish is a symbol for wealth and prosperity because the Chinese characters for "fish" and "abundance" have the same sound. People often use fish to express their longing for happiness.

因为“鱼”与“余”谐音，所以“鱼”在中国人心目中象征着财富有余、富贵昌盛，人们常常用“鱼”来表达自己对幸福的向往。

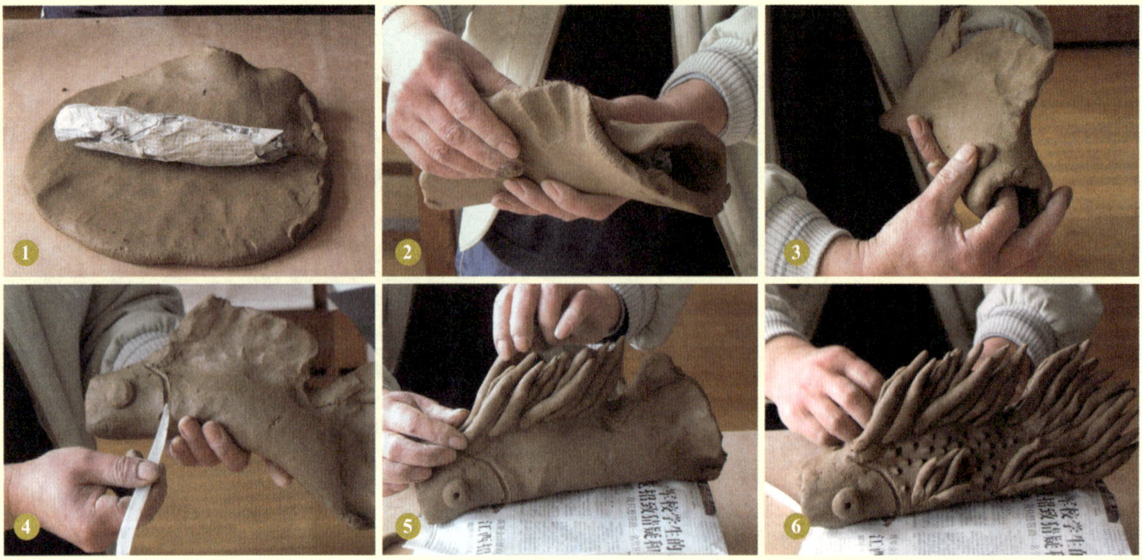

1 Make a round mud pie and use newspaper for the filling.
用手按压出一块圆形泥板，用报纸做填充物。

2 Make the shape of a fish.
捏出鱼的大体造型。

3 Make the eyes, gills and fins of the fish.
粘接鱼的眼睛、鱼鳃、鱼鳍等部位。

4 Make the mouth and teeth of the fish.
塑造鱼嘴，粘接牙齿等。

5 Make some thin mud bars (thick in the middle) and stick them to the gills.
随意搓出中间粗两头细的短泥条若干，粘于鱼鳍部位，形成流动的造型感。

6 Finish the fish and focus on the details.
完成造型，刻画细节。

Try It Yourself 试一试

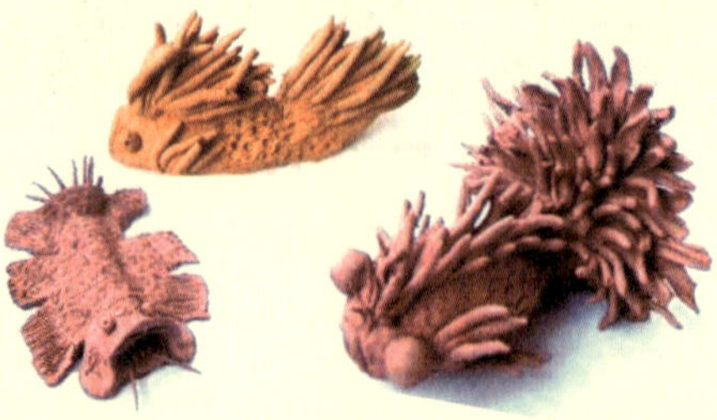

1. Create your own "auspicious fish" using your imagination or choose your favorite from the pictures on page 7. Follow the steps above and see whose work is the most creative.
参考上面的步骤图，发挥你的想象或在上页图片中选择一个你喜欢的造型，创作一个"吉祥的鱼"吧。比一比谁的作品最生动。

2. Try to make a fish-shaped pendant using a small piece of pottery clay.
试试看能不能用一小块陶土做出一个鱼形吊坠。

制作陶俑
Make a Pottery Figure

In ancient times, pottery figures or pottery sculptures were buried along with the dead. These have an important position among ancient sculptural works. Tens of kilometers east of Xi'an in Shaanxi Province, there is a grand underground "military army." This is called the world's eighth wonder – the Terracotta Warriors and Horses. In these archeological digs, over 8 000 Terracotta Warriors and Horses, the size of real ones, were discovered. These figures not only stand in accordance with their ranks and status but also have different clothes, hairstyles, body shapes and facial expressions. Even today we can sense the diverse experiences of each of these figures.

陶俑是中国古代用来陪葬的陶制塑像，在古代雕塑艺术品中占有重要的位置。在陕西省西安市往东数十公里处，有一座恢弘的地下军阵，这就是被称作世界第八大奇迹的秦始皇陵兵马俑。考古人员在秦始皇陵兵马俑坑中发现了8 000多个与真人真马一般大小的陶俑和陶马。这些陶俑不仅按照身份等级布阵排列，而且服饰、发型、体态、神情各不相同，似乎能令人感受到他们不同的遭遇和经历！

Guess 猜猜看

What rank in the army do the following figures belong to?

猜猜他们各自在军队中担任什么职责？

A.将军 General　　B.步兵 Infantry man

C.弓箭手 Archer　　D.驭手 Driver

1 Knead the shape of a person's face with your hand.
用手捏出一个人的面部形状。

2 Stick eyes onto the face.
粘接眼睛。

3 Make the mouth, beard, ears, etc.
塑造嘴巴、胡子、耳朵等部位。

4 Make the details of the hair and hairdressings.
塑造头饰和头发的细节。

5 Carve the details of the neck.
刻画颈部细节。

6 Complete modeling and continue to finish the details.
完成造型，刻画细节。

Try It Yourself 试一试

What kind of pottery figures do you like? Under the guidance of your teacher, complete your own pottery figure and see whose work is most life-like.

你喜欢什么样的陶俑？在老师的指导下做一个陶俑人像吧。比一比谁做的陶俑最生动。

Make a Pottery Tripod

制作陶鼎

The tripod was used in ancient times as an instrument for cooking, similar to a cauldron. Gradually it became a sacrificial vessel and was valued as the symbol of the founding of a state, representing the state and power. The tripod symbolized not only unification and peace but also prosperity and tranquility, thus is viewed as an auspicious sign.

鼎本来是古代的烹饪之器，相当于现在的锅，后来逐渐成为祭祀礼器，并因此而被视为立国重器，是国家和权力的象征。鼎不仅象征着统一与和平，还象征着昌盛与安宁，是吉祥之物。

Chinese Learning 汉语加油站

一言九鼎 yìyán jiǔdǐng
one word is more prized than nine tripods (one's words carry great weight)

大名鼎鼎 dàmíng dǐngdǐng
celebrated, preeminent, very famous

鼎盛时期 dǐngshèng shíqī
peak, prosperous time

鼎力相助 dǐnglì xiāngzhù
great support, generous help

1 Cut the clay tablet in proportion.
按比例切割泥板。

2 Make the body of the tripod with the cut clay tablet.
用切割好的泥板做成鼎身。

3 Paste on the tripod's legs.
粘上鼎的腿。

4 Paste on the four sides of the tripod.
粘好鼎口的四边。

5 Decorate the box of the tripod and paste the handles.
装饰鼎身，粘贴好鼎耳。

6 Finished.
整理完成。

Make a Pottery Dragon

制作陶龙

龙袍
Emperor's dragon robe

According to China's legends from the ancient times, the dragon is a miraculous animal that can change its form, create clouds and bring rains. Under the influence of mythology and legends, the Chinese people call themselves "descendants of the dragon."

In ancient China, the dragon is the symbol of the imperial power. Emperors of all dynasties considered themselves as incarnations of the dragon. There are phrases like "the true dragon and real son of heaven" and "the countenance of dragon (the emperor) is greatly pleased," etc. Utensils used by emperors were usually decorated with patterns of dragons.

龙是中国古代传说中善变化、能兴云雨的神异动物。在神话与传说的影响下，中国人也自称为“龙的传人”。

龙在中国古代还是皇权的象征，历代帝王都以龙自居，因此有“真龙天子”、“龙颜大悦”等词语，帝王使用的器物也多以龙为装饰。

剪纸
Paper-cut

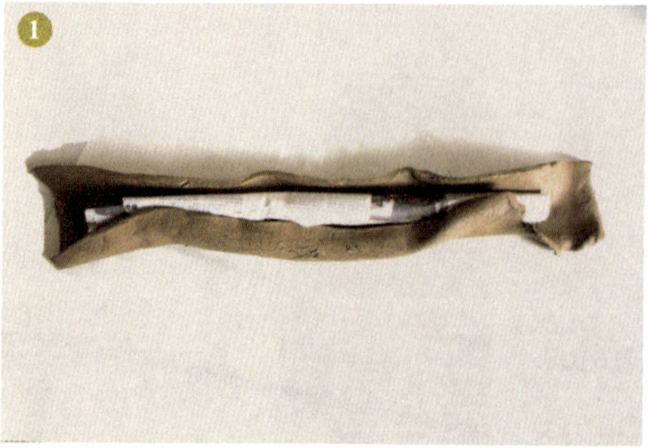

1 Make a rectangular clay tablet. Fill in the empty space with newspapers and roll it up like a thick tube-shaped object.
制作一块长方形泥板，用报纸填充，卷成筒状。

2 Hold the place to be pasted between the fingers and curve the body of the dragon.
把粘贴处捏薄立起，弯曲龙身。

3 Make the head and tail of the dragon.
做出龙头和龙尾部分。

4 Go on to draw and cut the other parts of the dragon.
深入刻画龙身的其他部分。

5 Cut patterns of clouds or water on another clay tablet, and place the finished dragon onto it.
在另一块泥板上简单刻画云或水的图案，把做好的龙放上去。

Make a Pottery House
制作陶房子

福建土楼
Tulou in Fujian Province

北京四合院
Siheyuan in Beijing

安徽民居
Building in Anhui Province

The civilian residence was an important part of China's traditional architecture in ancient times. Due to the various natural environments and living habits, traditional civilian residences in different regions of China are very diverse. There are many types of civilian residences which are unsophisticated and practical. These residences vividly reflect the harmonious relationship between man and nature.

民居是中国古代传统建筑中的重要组成部分。受自然环境和人文环境的影响，中国各地的传统民居建筑呈现出多样化的面貌，类型众多，古朴而实用，生动地反映了人与自然的和谐关系。

1 Cut out the shape of the ground, wall and roof from the clay tablet.
用泥板切割出地面、墙面和屋顶的形状。

2 Make the foundation of the house with clods and stick them well with mud.
用小泥块制作房屋的地基，用泥浆粘合住。

3 Stick the wall onto the foundation and make the four walls of the house.
将墙面粘接在地基上，搭好房子的四面墙。

4 Stick the roof onto the wall carefully and decorate it with pieces of clay.
将用泥条装饰过的屋顶小心地粘接在墙上。

5 Make the roof ridge and lay it across the cracks on the roof.
用泥条做出屋脊，弥合两边屋顶的缝隙。

6 When the main house is ready, make a smaller house beside it.
主屋做好后，在一旁做一个小屋。

7 Make the door threshold and entrance-way steps.
做出门槛和台阶。

8 Make two trees for decoration and place them in front of and behind the houses.
做两棵树作为点缀，置于屋前屋后。

制作陶狮子 Make a Pottery Lion

The stone lion is a commonly-seen decoration in China's traditional architecture in ancient times. It has been regarded as an auspicious sign. In the past, a pair of stone lions was placed in front of all the gates of government buildings, temples or great mansions to safeguard the houses. In modern times, we can also very often see two mighty stone lions at the gates of buildings.

石狮子是中国古代传统建筑中经常使用的装饰物，被视为吉祥之物。古代的官衙庙堂、豪门巨宅的大门前，都会摆放一对石狮子用以镇宅护卫。直到现代，在许多建筑物的大门前，你还会看到两只威武的石狮子。

Knowledge Links 知识链接

The placing of the stone lions has many rules. Usually the male lion is on the left and the female is on the right (in the direction of when a person is coming out of the gate). The male lion often has a ball made of strips of silk under his right front claw or holds the ball between his two front claws. The female lion often plays with a cub with her left front claw or has a cub between her two front claws.

石狮子的摆放是有规矩的，一般将雄狮摆放在左边，雌狮摆放在右边（以人从大门里出来的方向为参照）。雄狮一般都用右前爪玩绣球或两前爪之间放一个绣球，雌狮则用左前爪抚摸幼狮或两前爪之间卧一幼狮。

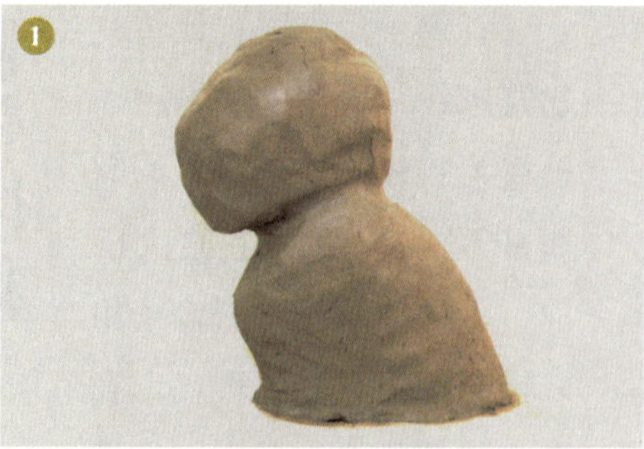

1 Knead two pieces of clay for the lion's head and body.
揉制两块泥团，分别做狮子的头和身体。

2 Make the lion's head and cut out the shape of the five facial features.
初步做出狮子的头和五官的形状。

3 Cut out the face and other features of the lion.
刻画狮子的五官特点和其他局部特征。

4 Make the lion's limbs and curly hair.
做出狮子的四肢和卷曲的头发。

5 Work the details until the lion is finished.
深入刻画直至完成。

Make a Pottery Eaves-tile

制作陶瓦当

"Eaves-tile" refers to the tile at the very front of the roof. It serves the function of protecting the roof of China's traditional architectural buildings in ancient times. The eaves-tile is often made of pottery, although sometimes it is made of cast iron, copper or colored glaze. The eaves-tile is usually decorated with patterns or characters on the surface. The two major shapes are round and semi-circle.

瓦当是屋檐最前端的一片瓦，在中国古代建筑中起着保护房檐的作用。瓦当的质地多为灰陶，也有铸铁、铜和琉璃材质的。瓦当表面多饰有图案、文字等，样式主要有圆形和半圆形两种。

1 Cut out a round clay tablet using a plate.
以盘子为模具切割出一个圆形泥板。

2 Draw a circle on the round clay tablet and draw some patterns in the circle (animals, flowers, grass, characters, etc.).
在圆泥板上画一个圆形，在圆内画出图形（可以是动物、花草、文字等）。

3 Get rid of the clay outside the patterns.
挖掉图形以外的泥。

4 Cut out the details and give the bottom of the tile some texture.
细致刻画，并做好底部的肌理。

Show Your Creativity
创意作品秀

Choose one thing you saw in China and make a similar one out of pottery. Put all your work together and see who made the most creative piece.

选一样你在中国见到的物品，把它做成陶艺作品展示给大家。比一比，谁的作品最有创意。

Answers 答 案

True or False? 判断正误 第2页

1. (T)　　2. (F)　　3. (F)

Guess 猜猜看 第5页

以瓷土为原料（ C ）　烧制温度较高（ C ）　敲击声音发闷（ T ）　不透明（ T ）

以陶土为原料（ T ）　烧制温度较低（ T ）　敲击声音清脆（ C ）　半透明（ C ）

瓷器：C　陶器：T

Guess 猜猜看 第9页

A.将军

D.驭手

B.步兵

C.弓箭手

图书在版编目（CIP）数据

学陶艺 / 国家汉办 / 孔子学院总部编著 . —北京：高等教育出版社，2011.6（2015.7重印）
《中国欢迎你》短期汉语系列教材 . 才艺类
ISBN 978-7-04-032804-2

Ⅰ . ①学…　Ⅱ . ①国…　Ⅲ . ①汉语—阅读教学—对外汉语教学—教学参考资料　Ⅳ . ① H195.4

中国版本图书馆 CIP 数据核字（2011）第 101720 号

策划编辑　周　芳　　责任编辑　鞠　慧　　封面设计　乔　剑　　版式设计　悦尔视觉
插图选配　鞠　慧　　责任校对　鞠　慧　刘映萩　　责任印制　朱学忠

出版发行　高等教育出版社
社　　址　北京市西城区德外大街4号
邮政编码　100120
印　　刷　北京信彩瑞禾印刷厂
开　　本　787×1092　1/16
印　　张　1.75
字　　数　44 000
购书热线　010-58581118
咨询电话　400-810-0598
网　　址　http://www.hep.edu.cn
　　　　　http://www.hep.com.cn
网上订购　http://www.landraco.com
　　　　　http://www.landraco.com.cn
版　　次　2011 年 6 月第 1 版
印　　次　2015 年 7 月第 5 次印刷
定　　价　13.80元

物 料 号　32804-00